1866-1991

125th

ANNIVERSARY

AND A WOODSTOCK IN A BIRCH TREE

by Charles M. Schulz

An Owl Book

Henry Holt and Company / New York

Published by Henry Holt and Company, Inc.,
115 West 18th Street, New York, New York 10011.
Published in Canada by Fitzhenry & Whiteside Limited,
195 Allstate Parkway, Markham, Ontario L3R 4T8.

Originally published in 1979 by Holt, Rinehart and Winston.

Library of Congress Catalog Card Number: 79-1926

ISBN 0-8050-1865-4 (An Owl Book: pbk.)

New Owl Book Edition—1991

Printed in the United States of America

Recognizing the importance of preserving the written word,
Henry Holt and Company, Inc., by policy, prints all of its
first editions on acid-free paper. ∞

1   3   5   7   9   10   8   6   4   2

WOODSTOCK, YOU'D HAVE MADE A GREAT CARRIER PIGEON! YOU COULD HAVE CARRIED MESSAGES BACK TO HEADQUARTERS...

IF YOU WERE CAPTURED, YOU WOULD REFUSE TO TALK EVEN IF YOU WERE TORTURED!

KLUNK!

WELL, MAYBE YOU COULD TALK A LITTLE...

OKAY, THIS IS YOUR FIRST FLIGHT AS A CARRIER PIGEON

I WANT YOU TO FLY FROM HERE TO THE COURTHOUSE

/!/!!
!!!?

WELL, IF YOU START TO GET LONELY, JUST COME ON BACK...

THERE ARE DIFFERENT WAYS OF TRAINING DOGS

I'VE BEEN READING ABOUT THE "SHAKE AND THROW" METHOD OF TRAINING PUPPIES...

A MOTHER DOG CAN'T HIT A PUPPY SO SHE PICKS IT UP, SHAKES IT AND THEN DROPS IT!

I CAN'T BELIEVE A PUPPY WOULD LEARN ANYTHING FROM THAT...

BONK!

ON THE OTHER HAND, I GUESS HE MIGHT LEARN A LITTLE..

LAST WEEK MY MOTHER SAID TO ME,"EUDORA, I THINK YOU SHOULD GO TO SUMMER CAMP!"

SO HERE I AM IN THE WILDERNESS

IT'S NOT TOO BAD...YOU MAY EVEN LIKE IT...

SO I'LL ASK YOU THE SAME THING I ASKED HER...

WHAT IF I GET EATEN BY AN ANTELOPE?

HEY, EUDORA, WE HAVE TO GO TO THE MAIN HALL FOR ORIENTATION!

IF THEY TRY TO SHIP US TO THE ORIENT, FORGET IT!

HOW DO YOU FEEL ABOUT WASHING DISHES AND SETTING TABLES?

I'D RATHER GO TO THE ORIENT!

SALLY, DO YOU BELIEVE IN UFO'S?

NO!

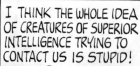

I THINK THE WHOLE IDEA OF CREATURES OF SUPERIOR INTELLIGENCE TRYING TO CONTACT US IS STUPID!

MY MOTHER TRIED TO CALL ME ON THE PHONE THIS MORNING

IF WE BECAME LOST IN THE WOODS, HOW LONG COULD WE GO WITHOUT REAL FOOD?

I'LL BET WE COULD GO FOR A MONTH WITHOUT REAL FOOD

HOW ABOUT JUNK FOOD?

ELEVEN MINUTES!

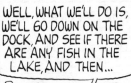

OKAY, EUDORA, YOU FISH IN THIS PART OF THE STREAM, AND I'LL FISH DOWN THERE IN THAT PART...

I DON'T THINK THIS IS GOING TO WORK

WHAT'S THE TROUBLE?

EITHER THE STREAM IS TOO NARROW, OR MY LINE IS TOO LONG...

THANK YOU FOR TEACHING ME ABOUT FISHING TODAY, SALLY... I HAD FUN!

I EVEN WROTE HOME TO MY DAD, AND TOLD HIM THAT I CAUGHT A BLUE MARLIN...

GOOD GRIEF! HE'LL NEVER BELIEVE A STORY LIKE THAT!

HE'LL BELIEVE IT... HE WANTS ME TO BE HAPPY...

I CAN'T BELIEVE THAT I WAS AWAY FROM HOME FOR TWO WEEKS

I NEVER THOUGHT I'D MAKE IT... I THOUGHT I'D CRACK UP...INSTEAD, I FEEL AS THOUGH I'VE MATURED...

THERE'S YOUR MOTHER WAITING FOR YOU AT THE BUS STOP...

SO MUCH FOR MATURITY!

WELL, I SUPPOSE YOU HAD YOUR USUAL MISERABLE TIME AT CAMP...DID YOU HATE IT?

UNFORTUNATELY, NO! I MET A NEW GIRL THERE NAMED EUDORA

I HAD TO KEEP CONVINCING HER THAT CAMP WAS FUN...

MY MISERABLE TIME WAS RUINED!!

OKAY, WE'LL RECEIVE ON THIS SIDE

THAT'S NOT FAIR!

THAT MEANS WE HAVE THE SUN IN OUR EYES! WHY DO WE ALWAYS SERVE WITH THE SUN IN OUR EYES?!

SEE? DIDN'T I TELL YOU? "CRYBABY" BOOBIE COMPLAINS ABOUT EVERYTHING!

I THINK THE NET IS TOO HIGH! THESE BALLS FEEL DEAD! I CAN'T PLAY ON A SLOW COURT! THESE BALLS ARE TOO LIVELY! I THINK THE NET IS TOO LOW!

HEY, "CRYBABY," WHY DON'T YOU SHUT UP AND SERVE?

THESE BALLS FEEL TOO LIGHT! MY SHOULDER HURTS! THE SUN IS KILLING ME! THE NET LOOKS TOO HIGH!

I SAID," SHUT UP AND SERVE!"

NOW YOU'RE TRYING TO PSYCHE ME OUT!!

BEATEN BY "CRYBABY" BOOBIE! WHAT A BLOW!

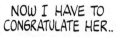

NOW I HAVE TO CONGRATULATE HER..

I DON'T KNOW WHY I PLAY THIS GAME..

CONGRATULATIONS, BOOBIE!

I'M SURE THIS LETTER IS FROM MY BROTHER SPIKE IN NEEDLES...

IT MUST BE IMPORTANT... IT HAS A THIRTEEN-CENT STAMP ON IT!

THE NAME ON THE STAMP SAYS CARL SANDBURG...

THAT'S GOTTA BE PANCHO GONZALES!

I HEAR YOUR BROTHER SPIKE IS COMING TO VISIT

NOT TO VISIT, TO **STAY**! THE COYOTES KICKED HIM OUT... HE HATES TO LEAVE NEEDLES...

ALTHOUGH, HE HASN'T FELT WELL LATELY... HE'S LOST WEIGHT AGAIN, AND HE'S BEEN DEPRESSED...

I KNOW THAT FEELING... I'M ALWAYS AFRAID I'M GOING TO OUTLIVE MY TEETH!

I HAVE AN IDEA

WHY DON'T WE TRY TO FIND A FAMILY AROUND HERE THAT WOULD ADOPT SPIKE?

CAN YOU THINK OF ANY REASON WHY SOMEONE MIGHT NOT WANT HIM?

WELL, HIS BACKHAND IS A LITTLE WEAK...

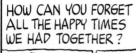

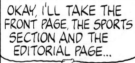

I DON'T KNOW WHY I EVEN KEEP YOU ON OUR TEAM...

I HAVE BOX OFFICE APPEAL, THAT'S WHY!

WE DON'T **HAVE** A BOX OFFICE!

IF YOU EVER GET A BOX OFFICE, I BET I'LL APPEAL TO IT!!

WELL, WE LOST AGAIN

LUCY, DO ME A FAVOR...

ASK OUR PLAYERS TO LINE UP TO SHAKE HANDS WITH THE OTHER TEAM AND SAY, "NICE GAME"

OKAY, TEAM, IT'S HYPOCRITE TIME!!

ALL RIGHT, TROOPS... BEFORE WE GO ON OUR HIKE, I'LL CALL THE ROLL

WOODSTOCK! CONRAD! BILL! OLIVIER!

ZZZZ

I SHOULD NEVER CALL THE ROLL BEFORE NOON!

DO YOU ALL SEE THAT HILL OVER THERE?

OUR OBJECTIVE TODAY IS TO CLIMB TO THE TOP OF THAT HILL...

ARE THERE ANY QUESTIONS? (/!!!!/ !!!!! !!! ?)

NO, CONRAD, I DON'T KNOW WHAT THE MEANING OF LIFE IS!

INCIDENTALLY, HOW DO YOU GUYS LIKE THE GRAPE JELLY I BROUGHT ALONG?

IT'S A NEW BRAND CALLED "SMIRK"

IF SOMEONE GETS JELLY ON HIS FACE, YOU CAN SAY TO HIM,"WIPE THAT 'SMIRK' OFF YOUR FACE!"

JUST A LITTLE JOKE THERE TO BOOST SAGGING MORALE

Z Z Z Z

OKAY, MEN, THE HIKE IS OVER... WE'RE HOME!

THIS IS WHERE YOU LIVE...WAKE UP!

Z Z Z Z

LET'S JUST SAY THAT LIFE HAS ME BEATEN...

SO I GIVE UP! I ADMIT THAT THERE'S NO WAY I CAN WIN...

WHAT IS IT YOU WANT, CHARLIE BROWN?

HOW ABOUT TWO OUT OF THREE?

RIDING AROUND ON THE BACK OF YOUR MOTHER'S BICYCLE IN THE HOT SUN IS NOT MY IDEA OF LIVING...

AT THE END OF THE DAY I FEEL LIKE A FRIED EGG...

THE ONLY THING THAT HELPS IS WHEN SHE ACCIDENTALLY DRIVES US THROUGH A..

...SPRINKLER!

HELLO? THIS IS MARCIE SPEAKING..

GOOD GRIEF! I DIALED THE WRONG NUMBER!

IS THAT YOU, CHUCK? IT SOUNDS LIKE YOUR VOICE...IF IT IS, HOW HAVE YOU BEEN?

IF IT ISN'T, WHAT DO I CARE HOW YOU'VE BEEN?

I'LL BET YOU DIALED MY NUMBER BY MISTAKE, DIDN'T YOU, CHUCK? I'LL BET YOU MEANT TO CALL PEPPERMINT PATTY...

SHE JUST HAPPENS TO BE RIGHT HERE BESIDE ME..I'LL PUT HER ON...

NO! WAIT! I...

HI, CHUCK! FINALLY GOT UP NERVE TO CALL ME, EH?

WHAT DID YOU WANT TO TALK TO ME ABOUT, CHUCK?

IF IT'S ABOUT GOING TO THE SHOW, WHY DON'T WE JUST MEET THERE AROUND ONE? THAT'LL SAVE YOU COMIN' CLEAR OVER HERE!

SEE YOU, CHUCK! GLAD YOU GOT OVER YOUR SHYNESS AND DECIDED TO CALL!

I CAN'T STAND IT...

WHERE ARE YOU GOING, BIG BROTHER?

WELL, I FINALLY GOT UP NERVE TO CALL THAT LITTLE RED-HAIRED GIRL, BUT I DIALED MARCIE BY MISTAKE, AND GOT A DATE WITH PEPPERMINT PATTY...

I THINK YOU'RE TOO WISHY-WASHY, BIG BROTHER

IT'S NOT A LOST ART!

I JUST SAW SOMETHING I'D LIKE TO HAVE FOR SCHOOL... A FIVE HUNDRED DOLLAR LUNCH BOX!

FIVE HUNDRED DOLLARS?!

THAT'S A LOT OF MONEY TO PAY FOR A LUNCH BOX

BUT WOULDN'T THE SANDWICHES TASTE GREAT?

CYRUS AND THE PERSIANS CAPTURED BABYLONIA...

THEN CAME ALEXANDER, WHO DRANK HIMSELF TO DEATH IN THE PALACE

I'M NOT SURE WHAT HAPPENED AFTER THAT

HOWEVER, I HOPE TO HAVE AN UPDATE FOR YOU VERY SOON

KING TIGLATH-PILESER OF ASSYRIA CONQUERED MANY NATIONS, AND CARRIED OFF THEIR BOOTY

THIS MEANT THAT NONE OF THE LITTLE BABIES HAD ANY BOOTIES

HA HA HA HA HA HA

IF IT HAD HAPPENED TO YOU, MAYBE YOU WOULDN'T BE LAUGHING!

SCHULZ

SCHOOL JUST STARTED AND ALREADY I SHOULD QUIT!

MY TEACHER YELLS AT ME, THE KIDS LAUGH AT ME AND THE PRINCIPAL HATES ME

WHAT ABOUT THE CUSTODIAN?

HE VACUUMED UP MY LUNCH!

SCHULZ

YES, MA'AM? YOU WANT ME TO WORK OUT THE PROBLEM AT THE BOARD?

WELL, LET'S SEE.. WE HAVE THESE NUMBERS HERE, DON'T WE?

4,678
× 52

THESE ARE NICE NUMBERS, MA'AM..

4,678
× 52

A FOUR, A SIX, A SEVEN, AN EIGHT, A FIVE AND A TWO

OH, YES, AND WE ALSO HAVE AN X ...

4,6
X

WELL, THE PROBLEM SEEMS TO BE TO TRY TO FIND OUT WHAT THIS X IS DOING AMONG ALL THESE NUMBERS...

IS HE AN OUT-SIDER? WAS HE INVITED TO JOIN THE GROUP? IT'S AN INTERESTING QUESTION...

4,6
X

LET'S FIND OUT WHAT THE REST OF THE CLASS THINKS... YOU THERE, IN THE THIRD ROW...WHAT DO YOU THINK ABOUT THIS? SPEAK UP!

MA'AM?

RATS! THREE MORE MINUTES AND THE BELL WOULD HAVE RUNG!

SCHULZ

Dear Grandma,
How are you? I am fine.

I have been working hard in school.

WHICH GRANDMA ARE YOU WRITING TO? WE HAVE TWO GRANDMAS, YOU KNOW...

I AM WELL AWARE OF THAT! I AM ALSO AWARE THAT THEY DON'T LIKE EACH OTHER...

AND THAT BRINGS UP A PROBLEM...

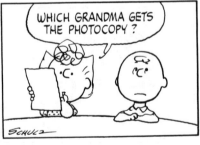

WHICH GRANDMA GETS THE PHOTOCOPY?

SCHULZ

NOW IT CAN BE TOLD..

I THINK I'VE DISCOVERED HOW MANY NOTCHES YOU CAN CUT INTO A DOGHOUSE BEFORE THE...

...ROOF FALLS IN!

THAT HAS TO BE THE DUMBEST EXPERIMENT I'VE EVER SEEN!

WHY WOULD ANYONE WANT TO KNOW HOW MANY NOTCHES YOU CAN PUT IN A DOGHOUSE BEFORE THE ROOF FALLS IN?

IT'S CALLED "LIVE AND LEARN"

OR IS IT "LIVE AND DON'T LEARN"?

PROBLEM NUMBER SIX...

"HOW MANY GALLONS OF CREAM CONTAINING 25% BUTTER FAT AND MILK CONTAINING $3\frac{1}{2}$% BUTTER FAT MUST BE MIXED TO..

..OBTAIN 50 GALLONS OF CREAM CONTAINING $12\frac{1}{2}$% BUTTER FAT?"

MA'AM, WOULD YOU SETTLE FOR TWENTY PUSH-UPS?

HERE COMES WOODSTOCK IN FOR A LANDING...

I CAN SEE ALREADY WHAT'S GOING TO HAPPEN..

TOO MUCH TOP SPIN!

"WERE YOU IN WHEN I CALLED?" SHE ASKED

"NO," HE SAID... "I WAS OUT AT THE INN!"

HEE HEE HEE HEE

WOODSTOCK LOVES INN JOKES!

"A Guide to Running"

Chapter One

How to run like a rabbit.

Hop Hop Hop Hop Hop Hop

MY NAME IS EUDORA, AND I'M NEW IN THIS CLASS

OUR FAMILY JUST MOVED HERE FROM OUT OF STATE

NO, MA'AM...I DON'T KNOW WHICH STATE

I DON'T EVEN KNOW WHERE I AM NOW!

WHAT ARE YOU EATING FOR LUNCH, EUDORA?

THIS IS A CHOCOLATE SANDWICH

I PUT A CHOCOLATE BAR BETWEEN TWO SLICES OF DARK BREAD

I OFTEN WONDER HOW IT WOULD TASTE WITH GRAVY ON IT...

OH, YOU'RE A FINE ONE, YOU ARE! I'VE ALWAYS BEEN NICE TO YOU, BUT DID YOU CARE?

NO, YOU DIDN'T! AND NOW A NEW GIRL MOVES IN AND SMILES ONCE AT YOU, AND YOU GIVE HER YOUR BLANKET!

OH, YOU'RE A FINE ONE YOU ARE! YOU KNOW WHAT I HOPE? I HOPE YOU HAVE A NERVOUS BREAKDOWN, THAT'S WHAT I HOPE!!

YOU MUST BE A GOOD HOPER...

STILL HAVE MY BLANKET, I SEE...

OH, YES... I FIND IT A GREAT SOURCE OF COMFORT AND SECURITY

THANK YOU FOR GIVING IT TO ME, SWEET BABBOO...

HE'S NOT YOUR SWEET BABBOO!!

SNOOPY, I NEED YOUR HELP

I GAVE MY BLANKET TO EUDORA, AND I WANT YOU TO GET IT BACK FOR ME...I DON'T CARE HOW YOU DO IT!

HMMM...

HERE'S THE WORLD FAMOUS DISCO DANCER ABOUT TO CHARM HIS WAY INTO A CHICK'S HEART...

YOU ASKED SNOOPY TO GET YOUR BLANKET BACK FROM EUDORA?

IF ANYONE CAN DO IT, HE CAN...HE'S GOING TO WIN HER OVER AT THE DISCO SCENE

THE DISCO SCENE?

HI, BABE! DO YOU COME HERE OFTEN?

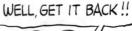

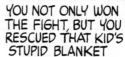

THIS IS MY REPORT ON BAKERIES...

A GIRL WENT INTO A BAKERY AND ASKED, "DO YOU SERVE BIG COOKIES IN HERE?"

"I DON'T KNOW," SAID THE BAKER... "HOW TALL ARE YOU?"
HA HA HA HA HA

WELL, BAKERS HAVE TO HAVE FUN, TOO, YOU KNOW, MA'AM!

LEARN FROM YESTERDAY

LIVE FOR TODAY

LOOK TO TOMORROW

REST THIS AFTERNOON

"a lopsided man runs fastest along the little side-hills of success."

WHO SAID THAT, MOSES?

NO, A MAN NAMED FRANK MOORE COLBY...

IT SOUNDS LIKE SOMETHING MOSES WOULD HAVE SAID...

ACTUALLY, IT DOESN'T SOUND AT ALL LIKE SOMETHING MOSES WOULD HAVE SAID!

HOW DO YOU KNOW? YOU NEVER TALKED TO MOSES, DID YOU?

MOSES LIKED TO SAY THINGS LIKE THAT!

IF MOSES HAD THOUGHT OF IT, MOSES WOULD HAVE SAID IT!

NO, YOU'RE TOO SMALL TO SWING IN AN OLD TIRE LIKE THAT

YOU NEED SOMETHING MORE YOUR SIZE...

LIKE A GLAZED DOUGHNUT!

THAT'S HOW MANY PIZZAS WE'VE EATEN BEFORE MIDNIGHT

NOW, WE'LL ADD THAT TO HOW MANY PIZZAS WE'VE EATEN AFTER MIDNIGHT, AND...

POOF!

THAT BLEW MY POCKET CALCULATOR!

MAYBE, WHEN YOU GET TO BE A FAMOUS BASEBALL PLAYER, CHARLIE BROWN, THEY'LL NAME A CANDY BAR AFTER YOU...

YEAH! WOULDN'T THAT BE GREAT?

I'M VERY FLATTERED THAT YOU SHOULD THINK OF SUCH A THING

IT'LL PROBABLY BE HARD TO UNWRAP AND HAVE CHOCOLATE THAT MELTS ALL OVER YOUR FINGERS

WOODSTOCK IS INTO MACRAMÉ

HE'S ALSO INTO RUNNING, AND HE'S INTO POETRY

HE'S INTO MEDITATION, AND HE'S INTO GENEALOGY

ACTUALLY, HE'S INTO "INTO"!

YOU NEVER HAVE ANY SELF-DOUBTS, DO YOU?

ME?

HAHAHAHA!!

NO, I GUESS NOT

I DON'T UNDERSTAND YOUR QUESTION, CHARLIE BROWN...WHY SHOULD I HAVE SELF-DOUBTS?

WHY NOT? AFTER ALL, YOU'RE NOT REALLY PERFECT, YOU KNOW

I'VE NEVER SEEN ANYONE SO OFFENDED!

THE WEATHER MAY GET WORSE, MEN

IS ANYONE WORRIED? DO YOU ALL KNOW HOW TO ACT IN A BLIZZARD? DOES ANYONE HAVE A QUESTION ABOUT ANYTHING?

NO, OLIVIER, I DON'T THINK THERE'S A PLACE AROUND HERE WHERE YOU CAN MAIL YOUR POST CARDS

YES, BILL, I'VE MET CHERYL TIEGS...YES, SHE'S VERY NICE..

SHOPPING DAYS? WELL, CONRAD, I'D GUESS THERE ARE ABOUT TWENTY-FOUR MORE SHOPPING DAYS UNTIL CHRISTMAS

ANY MORE QUESTIONS?

NO, WOODSTOCK, I DON'T KNOW WHY YOU'RE STANDING HERE IN A BLIZZARD WITH THESE THREE IDIOTS...

I DIDN'T THINK I WAS EVER GOING TO GET A SENSIBLE QUESTION

SCHULZ

WHAT ARE YOU PACING AROUND FOR CHARLIE BROWN?

I'M WORRIED, I GUESS

I'M WORRIED ABOUT MY DOG...

HE TOOK HIS BEAGLE SCOUTS BACKPACKING, AND I'M AFRAID HE MAY BE LOST IN THIS SNOWSTORM...

IF THEY ALL FOLLOW HIM, THEY'RE SURE TO GET LOST!

THAT STUPID BEAGLE COULDN'T FIND HIS WAY ACROSS THE KITCHEN FLOOR!

I DON'T KNOW...I SORT OF HAD THE IDEA HE WAS AN EXPERT AT GETTING AROUND IN THE WOODS...

NOW, THE DIRECTION WE WANT TO LOCATE IS WEST...THEREFORE, WE SIMPLY LOOK FOR THE MOON, KNOWING AS WE DO THAT THE MOON IS ALWAYS OVER HOLLYWOOD, AND THAT HOLLYWOOD IS IN THE WEST...

SCHULZ

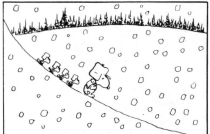

IN MY BOOK ABOUT BEETHOVEN, I'VE MADE A FEW IMPROVEMENTS

FOR INSTANCE, INSTEAD OF PLAYING THE PIANO, I HAVE HIM PLAYING AN ELECTRIC GUITAR...

ALSO, IN MY BOOK HE DOESN'T HAVE STOMACH PAINS..

I'VE UPDATED IT TO TENNIS ELBOW!

I HATE TO SHOW ANY INTEREST, BUT IN YOUR BOOK, DOES BEETHOVEN MEET ANY OTHER WOMEN?

OH, YES! IN CHAPTER FOUR HIS LANDLADY SAYS TO HIM, "IF YOU DON'T PAY YOUR RENT, YOU KNOW WHAT I'LL DO?"

"I'LL KICK YOUR PIANO!"

I KNEW I SHOULDN'T HAVE SHOWN ANY INTEREST...

I MAILED MY MANUSCRIPT YESTERDAY.. SO WHAT HAPPENS? ZERO!

MY BOOK ISN'T IN ANY OF THE STORES OR ON A SINGLE BEST-SELLER LIST! WHAT A DISAPPOINT- MENT! WHAT A BLOW!

YOU'RE THE MOST IMPATIENT AUTHOR I'VE EVER SEEN...

OH, YEAH? WELL, WHAT ABOUT MY ROYALTY STATEMENT? WHERE'S MY ROYALTY STATEMENT?

HAPPY BEETHOVEN'S BIRTHDAY!

THANK YOU

IT WOULD BE A LOT BETTER IF EVERYONE HAD MY BOOK TO READ

I LOVED THE PART WHERE I TELL ABOUT HOW HE PLAYED FOR LINCOLN'S INAUGURAL BALL

HAPPY BEETHOVEN'S BIRTHDAY

I THINK YOU SAID THAT!

"LITTLE GEORGE WAS WAITING FOR SANTA TO COME"

"SUDDENLY HE HEARD THE SOUND OF SOMEONE WALKING ON THE ROOF! IT WAS A MAN IN A YELLOW SLICKER AND BIG RUBBER BOOTS!"

"'I SAW HIM!' SHOUTED LITTLE GEORGE.. 'I SAW SANTA AND HIS RAIN GEAR'"

DON'T SQUIRM, MA'AM, THERE'S MORE TO COME!

"THE RAIN CAME DOWN HARDER AND HARDER"

"BUT THE MAN IN THE YELLOW SLICKER AND BIG RUBBER BOOTS NEVER FALTERED"

"ANOTHER CHRISTMAS EVE HAD PASSED, AND SANTA AND HIS RAIN GEAR HAD DONE THEIR JOB! THE END"

HA HA HA! HA HA! HA HA!

A FINE BROTHER YOU ARE! YOU LET ME MAKE A FOOL OUT OF MYSELF!!

IT ISN'T RAIN GEAR! IT'S REINDEER! WHY DIDN'T YOU TELL ME?!

THEY ALL LAUGHED AT ME! EVEN THE TEACHER LAUGHED AT ME! I'LL NEVER BE ABLE TO GO TO THAT SCHOOL AGAIN!

POOR SWEET BABY...

SNIF!

THEY SURE HAD THEIR NERVE LAUGHING AT MY STORY.... HA!

HOW ABOUT THIS THING WITH ALL THE REINDEER PULLING THE SLEIGH THROUGH THE AIR? NO WAY!

I DON'T CARE HOW MANY REINDEER HE HAD, THEY COULD NEVER PRODUCE ENOUGH LIFT TO GET A SLED IN THE AIR...

NO WAY, HUH, BIG BROTHER?

NO WAY! MERRY CHRISTMAS!

THERE'S THE HOUSE WHERE THAT LITTLE RED-HAIRED GIRL LIVES...

MAYBE SHE'LL SEE ME, AND COME RUSHING OUT TO THANK ME FOR THE CHRISTMAS CARD I SENT HER...MAYBE SHE'LL EVEN GIVE ME A HUG...

MAYBE BILLIE JEAN KING WILL CALL ME TONIGHT, AND INVITE ME OUT TO DINNER

WHY ARE YOU HIDING BEHIND THIS TREE, CHARLIE BROWN?

I'M JUST LOOKING AT THE HOUSE WHERE THE LITTLE RED-HAIRED GIRL LIVES..UNFORTUNATELY, SHE DOESN'T KNOW I'M ALIVE

WHAT YOU NEED THEN IS SOME SUBTLE WAY OF LETTING HER KNOW

I GUESS THAT'S RIGHT

HEY, KID, YOUR LOVER'S OUT HERE!

IT'S A NEW COURSE...
I THINK IT'S JUST
WHAT I NEED

AS SOON AS I SAW
IT ON THE LIST, I
SIGNED UP...

WHAT'S IT CALLED?

REMEDIAL LIVING!

A NEW YEAR'S
TOAST!

TO THAT WONDERFUL
GENIUS...

TO THAT PERSON
WE ALL ADMIRE...

THE INVENTOR OF
THE DOGGIE BAG!

Deer

THAT SHOULD BE "DEAR"

IN THE SALUTATION OF A LETTER, THE PROPER WORD AND SPELLING OF THAT WORD IS "DEAR"

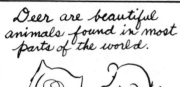

Deer are beautiful animals found in most parts of the world.

I'M SORRY... I DIDN'T REALIZE YOU WERE WRITING ABOUT DEER... I APOLOGIZE...

WELL, I SHOULD HOPE SO! IT SEEMS TO ME THAT A LOT OF THE PROBLEMS IN THIS WORLD ARE CAUSED BY PEOPLE WHO CRITICIZE OTHER PEOPLE BEFORE THEY KNOW WHAT THEY'RE TALKING ABOUT!

Dear Grandma,

PRACTICING YOUR I'S, I SEE

THESE AREN'T I'S... THESE ARE OCEAN WAVES!

THERE'S A TINY SEA GULL FLYING OVER EACH WAVE

I WAS JUST FOOLING YOU... ACTUALLY, I WAS LYING! I'M PRACTICING TO BE A SPY, AND THIS IS A CODE I'VE WORKED OUT

IF I'M CAPTURED WITH THIS PAPER, I COULD EVEN TELL THEM IT'S A DRAWING OF A ROW OF LOW-FLYING BEES ZOOMING OVER BLADES OF GRASS!

WHAT IF YOU'RE TORTURED?

TORTURED?

YOU'RE RIGHT! IT'S A ROW OF I'S!

THIS IS KIND OF INTERESTING..

"AN EARTHQUAKE IS A SHAKING MOVEMENT OF THE EARTH'S SURFACE"

"THEY ARE MOST COMMONLY CAUSED BY THE JAR GIVEN THE EARTH'S SURFACE WHEN A FAULT OCCURS"

"STUDY OF EARTHQUAKES HELPS US TO LEARN MORE ABOUT THE NATURE OF THE EARTH'S INTERIOR"

"EVERYONE SHOULD KNOW WHAT TO DO IF AN EARTHQUAKE OCCURS"

"THE SAFEST PLACE TO STAND DURING AN EARTHQUAKE IS IN A DOORWAY"

SNOOPY

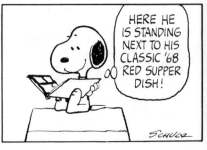

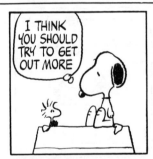

IT'S HARD TO CHEER UP A DEPRESSED BIRD

YOU NEED A GIRL FRIEND, THAT'S WHAT YOU NEED

WHY DON'T YOU GO HANG AROUND SOME TELEPHONE WIRES? OR BETTER YET, JOIN A WORM GROUP!

A WORM GROUP! THAT'S A GOOD ONE! HEE HEE HEE HEE HEE!

I'M SORRY! HEE HEE HEE HEE! I ALWAYS LAUGH! HEE HEE HEE!

HEY, WHAT DO YOU THINK YOU'RE DOING?

BUILDING A SNOWMAN

BUT HE'S UPSIDE DOWN!

A SNOWMAN IS SUPPOSED TO BE FUN TO LOOK AT

NO ONE IS GOING TO **CARE** ABOUT A SNOWMAN WHO'S UPSIDE DOWN!

HOW QUAINT!

HOW YOU SPEND YOUR TIME IS VERY IMPORTANT...

PSYCHIATRIC HELP 25¢
THE DOCTOR IS IN

A PERSON'S ACTIVITIES SAY A LOT ABOUT HIM, CHARLIE BROWN

WHAT HAVE YOU DONE SO FAR TODAY?

WELL, I SPENT MOST OF THE MORNING CLEANING OFF THE TOP OF MY DRESSER...

GOOD GRIEF!! PEOPLE ALL AROUND THE WORLD ARE PLOWING FIELDS, CHOPPING WOOD, DIGGING WELLS, PLANTING TREES, LAYING BRICKS, AND ALL YOU'VE DONE IS CLEAN THE TOP OF YOUR DRESSER?!!

NO WONDER YOU HAVE NO FEELING OF SELF-WORTH!

HEY, YOU THERE! WHAT HAVE YOU BEEN DOING TODAY?
THE DOCTOR IS IN

WATCHING TV, WHY?

THE TOP OF MY DRESSER IS REAL CLEAN!
THE DOCTOR IS IN

FIFTEEN TIMES SEVEN? HMM...

PSST! WHAT DID YOU PUT DOWN FOR THE THIRD QUESTION, SIR?

I PUT DOWN "GREEN"

GREEN?!

BUT THE QUESTION WAS, "HOW MUCH IS FIFTEEN TIMES SEVEN?"

I THOUGHT MAYBE IT WAS A TRICK QUESTION!

HERE'S A BOOK ABOUT PIRATES, SIR

YOU MEAN GUYS WHO STEAL OTHER PEOPLE'S RECORDINGS?

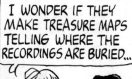

I WONDER IF THEY MAKE TREASURE MAPS TELLING WHERE THE RECORDINGS ARE BURIED...

YOU'RE HOPELESS, SIR!

♪"KISS ME ONCE AND KISS ME TWICE..THEN KISS ME ONCE AGAIN... IT'S BEEN A LONG LONG TIME..." ♪

SHH!! YOU HAVE TO BE QUIET IN A LIBRARY, SIR!

JUST SINGING AN OLD WORLD WAR II SONG, MARCIE...

BET IT BROUGHT BACK A FLOOD OF MEMORIES, HUH, MA'AM?

I CAN'T HELP YOU WITH YOUR HOMEWORK BECAUSE I HAVE MY OWN HOMEWORK TO DO...

IF YOU DON'T HELP ME, I'LL BUMP YOUR ELBOW SO YOU CAN'T WRITE STRAIGHT

I'LL BUMP YOUR NOSE!

THESE ARE EASY PROBLEMS

A GOOD WATCHDOG SHOULD BE WELL FED

THAT'S WHY I DON'T MIND FIXING YOU A GOOD DINNER EVERY NIGHT

I REALIZE THAT A WATCHDOG SOMETIMES HAS TO GO INTO ACTION AT A MOMENT'S NOTICE...

NOT ME...I NEED AT LEAST TWO WEEKS TO PLAN MY STRATEGY!